Yummy Crochet

Kristi Simpson

LEISURE ARTS, INC. • Maumelle, Arkansas

Be
KIND

Introduction

A few years ago, I was given a very old box of Workbasket books that were owned by my Great Grandmother. After her passing, they were stored and passed from family member to family member – and I was so excited to be gifted this box as a family member was cleaning out her closet. I love looking at them! They have a fun mix of old advertising ideas mixed with random crochet or knitting patterns. There were some that were full pattern booklets and they were so unique! They range from the 1950's to 1980's...Some are written in and others obviously used. Definitely a treasure to keep.

As I looked through them, I was inspired by one of the repeating themes. They usually had a recipe and then a set of patterns. They didn't really go together BUT my creative brain began to create a book of small recipes paired with dishcloths to match. For instance, if you have a cherry pie, you'd have a cherry dishcloth. And if you had a chicken dish, you'd have a chicken dishcloth... Fun things that have a dual audience! And for the crocheter, they would have a multi-function book. Recipes and patterns!

So, sit back and enjoy your mug of Hot Cocoa and crochet a fun dishcloth, while your Beefy Gumbo is in the crock pot and your Mile High Apple Pie is in the oven! This book will be fun to work and cook through!

About the Recipes

I was raised with all of the 'fixins' in the kitchen.... veggies, fried chicken, lots of calories. The 'good' stuff. Trust me, we had the boxed meals and mac and cheese as well as the home cooked meals, but my favorite meals were ones with the whole extended family and unique dishes. I am very close to my family and I must give a huge shout out to a few who pitched in Yummy recipes! Let's start with my favorite Aunt Kaye (just FYI, I call all of them my 'favorite'!). She is on my speed dial for 'HELP WITH A RECIPE'. Seriously, if I need help knowing when to 'fold' or 'whisk' or need to know a sugar substitution, she's my 'go-to'. Now, my favorite Aunt Faye (they're twins!) is on my speed dial for 'HELP WITH DINNER'. She is full of ideas and always brings tasty ideas to my table! I narrowed my recipes down to match my dishcloths and then I called my Mom (Mary). I said, "I need a recipe that will go with the flower dishcloth". This might be my favorite part....she said, "Squash has a flower when it blooms!" I snagged her squash and zucchini casserole recipe and I just know you're going to love it!

Now, you're in luck because with their help and my beautiful Mom (Mary), we have tested and TASTED our way through this book and not only am I excited about all of these recipes and pattern...but I'm full! HA!
I hope that you enjoy making these recipes, crocheting the dishcloths, and love them as much as I do!

Kristi

MEET Kristi Simpson

Inspired by her love of yarn, Kristi enjoys designing knit and crochet patterns with a fresh and modern touch. By using a mix of stitches creatively, she designs patterns that are great for beginners and beyond. She also had many books published with more in the works, featured as host in several video tutorials and been included in multiple magazines.

Look for other Leisure Arts books featuring Kristi's designs at *www.leisurearts.com/meet-the-designers/kristi-simpson.html*

Table of Contents

Barn

●●○○ **EASY**

Finished Size:
Approximately 10½" (26.5 cm) square

SHOPPING LIST

Yarn (Medium Weight) MEDIUM 4

[2.65 ounces, 131 yards
(75 grams, 120 meters) per skein]:

- ☐ Cream (Color A) - 1 skein
  OR 105 yards (96 meters)
- ☐ Burgundy (Color B) - 1 skein
  OR 35 yards (32 meters)

Crochet Hook

- ☐ Size G (4 mm)
  or size needed for gauge

Additional Supplies

- ☐ Yarn needle

GAUGE INFORMATION

In chart pattern,
16 sc and 18 rows = 4" (10 cm)

Gauge Swatch: 4" (10 cm) square
Ch 17.

Row 1: Sc in second ch from hook and in each ch across.

Rows 2-18: Ch 1, turn; sc in each sc across.

Finish off.

Note: Entire dishcloth is made with sc ***(see Basic Stitches, page 47)***.

DISHCLOTH

With Color A, ch 46.

Row 1 (Right side)**:** Sc in second ch from hook and in each ch across: 45 sc.

Note: Loop a short piece of yarn around any stitch to mark Row 1 as **right** side.

Rows 2-4: Ch 1, turn; sc in each sc across.

To change colors, work sc **before** color change to the last step (2 loops on hook), yarn over with the new color and draw through both loops on hook ***(Fig. A)***, dropping the old color. Work over dropped color as you work the row ***(Fig. B)***.

Fig. A

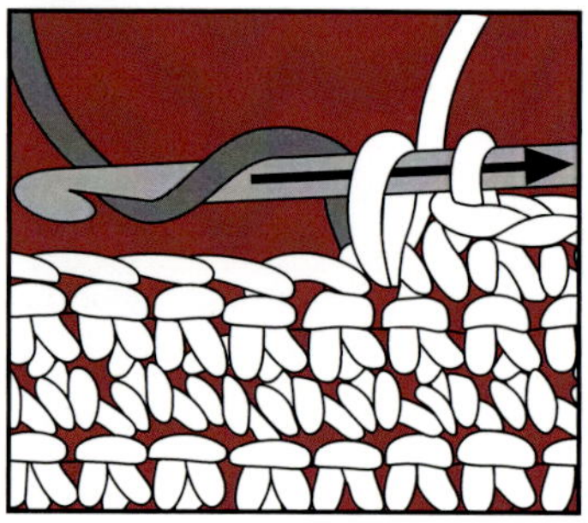

Fig. B

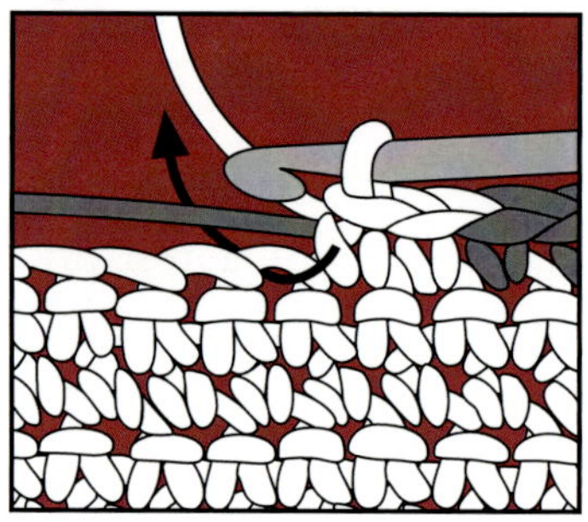

Row 5: Ch 1, turn; sc in first 8 sc changing to Color B in last sc, with Color B sc in next 28 sc changing to Color A in last sc, with Color A sc in last 9 sc.

Rows 6-45: Following Chart on page 8 for color changes, continue to work in sc; cut Color B after working Row 41; do **not** finish off.

Trim

Rnd 1: With Color A ch 1, do **not** turn; working in end of rows, skip first row, sc in next 43 rows, skip last row; working in free loops of beginning ch ***(Fig. 1, page 47)***, 3 sc in first ch, sc in next 43 chs, 3 sc in next ch; working in end of rows, skip first row, sc in next 43 rows, skip last row; 3 sc in first sc of Row 45, sc in next 43 sc, 3 sc in last sc; join with slip st to first sc, finish off: 184 sc.

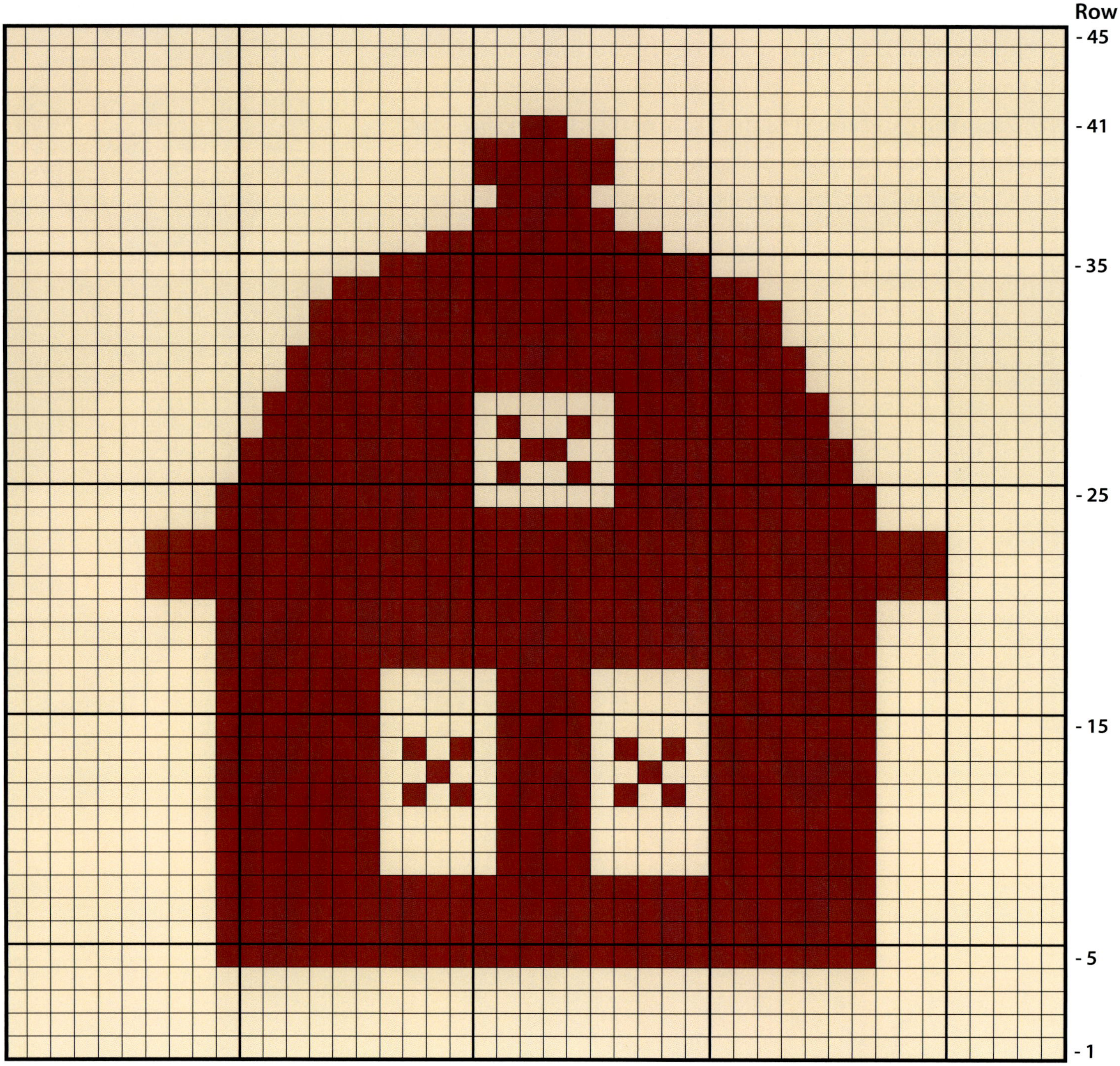

CHART

Work from **right** to **left** on right side rows; work from **left** to **right** on wrong side rows.

KEY

Color A

Color B

Beefy Gumbo

Recipe from Kaye Goens

Prep Time: 20 minutes

Chop! Chop! Chop! *This yummy recipe is perfect for veggie lovers and for crocheters. Once you mix up your gumbo, you'll have plenty of time to crochet...until the crock pot timer dings! Then you'll run to the kitchen! I promise this will be your go-to for yarn and veggie stash.*

Directions:

1. In a medium skillet, brown the ground beef over medium heat until full cooked, 7 to 9 minutes, stirring often to break up the meat. Pour off any standing liquid.
2. Combine all ingredients in crock pot and cook on high 4-6 hours, or until vegetables are tender.

Ingredients:

1 lb ground beef (80% lean)
1 medium onion, chopped
1 stalk celery, thinly sliced
2 medium carrots, sliced
1 (8.75 ounce) can whole kernel corn, drained
1 bag frozen mixed vegetables (I prefer gumbo variety)
1 (14 ounce) can diced tomatoes
1 (15 ounce) can tomato sauce
1 (32 ounce) carton beef broth
½ teaspoon garlic powder
½ teaspoon onion salt
Salt and pepper to taste
½ teaspoon cayenne (optional)

Bee Kind

●●○○ EASY

Finished Size: Approximately 10½" (26.5 cm) square

SHOPPING LIST

Yarn (Medium Weight) MEDIUM 4

[2.65 ounces, 131 yards (75 grams, 120 meters) per skein]:

- ☐ Yellow (Color A) - 1 skein
  OR 125 yards (114.5 meters)
- ☐ Black (Color B) - 1 skein
  OR 30 yards (27.5 meters)

Crochet Hook

- ☐ Size G (4 mm)
  or size needed for gauge

Additional Supplies

- ☐ Yarn needle

GAUGE INFORMATION

In chart pattern,
16 sc and 18 rows = 4" (10 cm)

Gauge Swatch: 4" (10 cm) square

Ch 17.

Row 1: Sc in second ch from hook and in each ch across.

Rows 2-18: Ch 1, turn; sc in each sc across.

Finish off.

Note: Entire dishcloth is made with sc ***(see Basic Stitches, page 47)***.

DISHCLOTH

With Color A, ch 46.

Row 1 (Right side): Sc in second ch from hook and in each ch across: 45 sc.

Note: Loop a short piece of yarn around any stitch to mark Row 1 as **right** side.

Rows 2-6: Ch 1, turn; sc in each sc across.

To change colors, work sc **before** color change to the last step (2 loops on hook), yarn over with the new color and draw through both loops on hook ***(Fig. A)***, dropping the old color. Work over dropped color as you work the row ***(Fig. B)***.

Fig. A

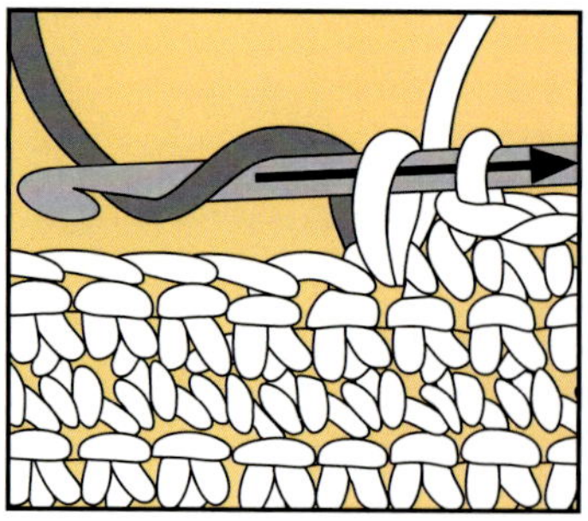

Fig. B

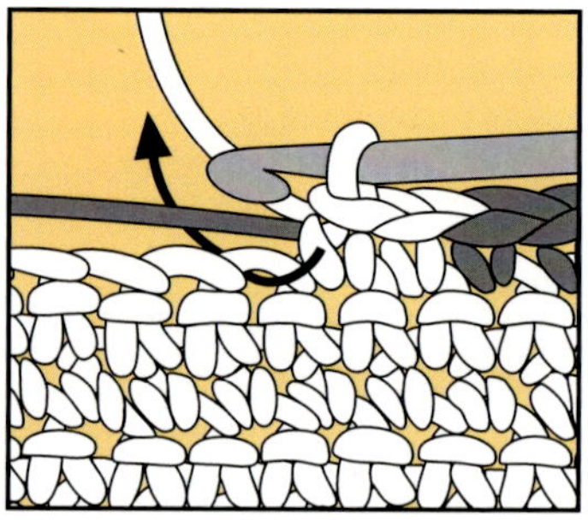

Row 7: Ch 1, turn; sc in first 7 sc changing to Color B in last sc, with Color B sc in next 5 sc changing to Color A in last sc, with Color A sc in next 2 sc, with Color B sc in next 3 sc, with Color A sc in next 3 sc, with Color B sc in next 3 sc, with Color A sc in next 2 sc, with Color B sc in next 4 sc, with Color A sc in next 2 sc, with Color B sc in next 3 sc, with Color A sc in next 3 sc, with Color B sc in next 3 sc, with Color A sc in last 5 sc.

Rows 8-45: Following Chart on page 12 for color changes, continue to work in sc; cut Color B after working Row 40; do **not** finish off.

Trim

Rnd 1: With Color A ch 1, do **not** turn; working in end of rows, skip first row, sc in next 43 rows, skip last row; working in free loops of beginning ch ***(Fig. 1, page 47)***, 3 sc in first ch, sc in next 43 chs, 3 sc in next ch; working in end of rows, skip first row, sc in next 43 rows, skip last row; 3 sc in first sc of Row 45, sc in next 43 sc, 3 sc in last sc; join with slip st to first sc, finish off: 184 sc.

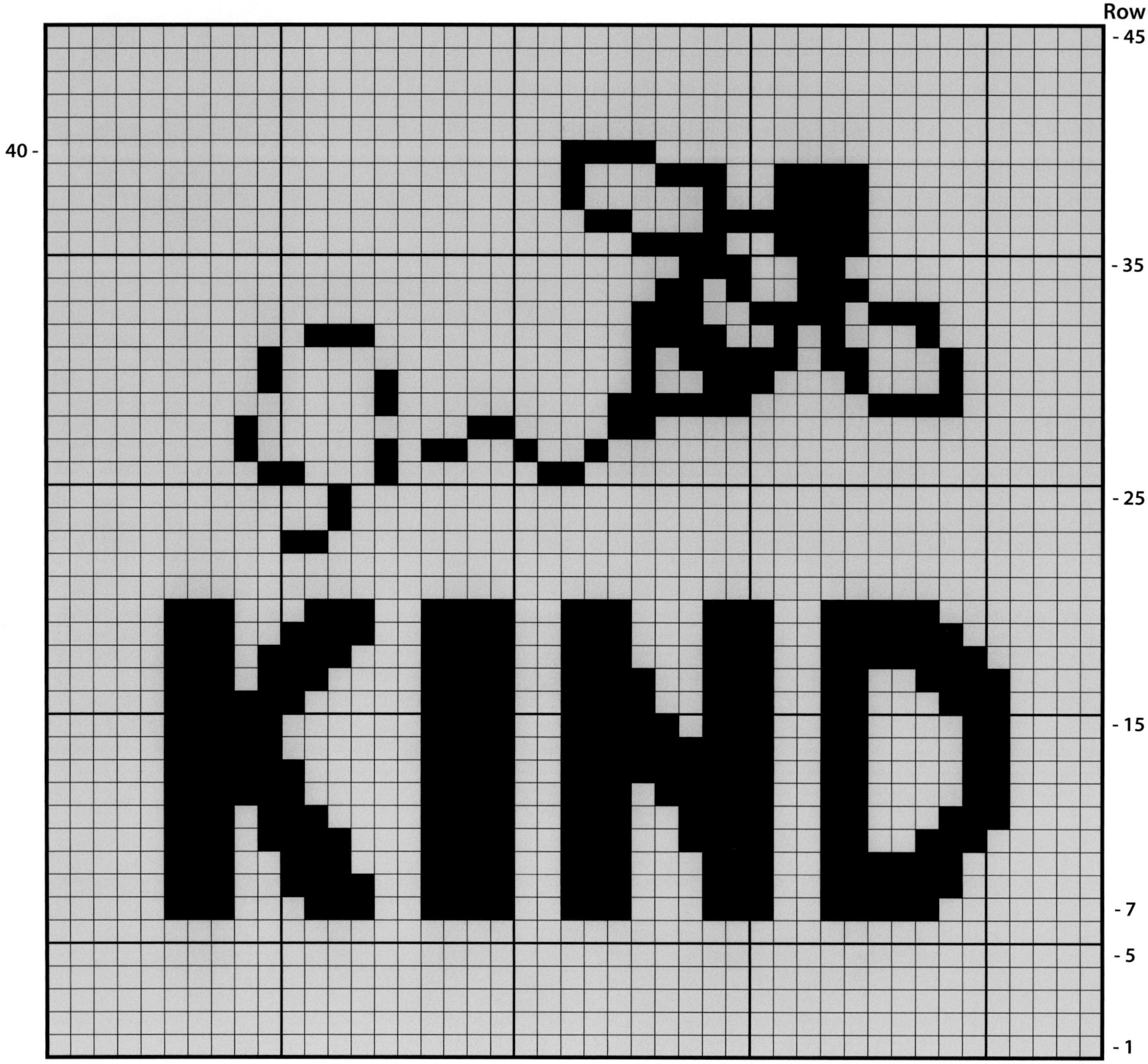

CHART

Work from **right** to **left** on right side rows; work from **left** to **right** on wrong side rows.

KEY

Color A

Color B

Honey Mustard Dipping Sauce

Recipe from Faye Forton

Prep Time: 5 minutes

Honey mustard is amazing and so tasty, and it's homemade! You won't believe how simple it is...but you have to have THIS recipe! This was made with trial and error over 20 different times until it was perfect. You'll love how creamy it is and that it makes enough for now...and later.
Note: Aunt Faye please make Uncle Bob his own bowl of Honey Mustard for the Sausage Balls so he doesn't pout!

Ingredients:

1 cup mayo (I prefer Hellman's®)
1 tablespoon of Kraft Sweet 'n Sour Sauce
2 teaspoons yellow mustard
1 tablespoon honey

Directions:

1. In a large bowl, whisk together all ingredients.
2. Store leftovers in a covered container in the refrigerator for up to 4 days.

Chicken

●●○○ **EASY**

Finished Size:
Approximately 10½" (26.5 cm) square

SHOPPING LIST

Yarn (Medium Weight)

[2.65 ounces, 131 yards (75 grams, 120 meters) per skein]:

- ☐ Grey (Color A) - 1 skein
  OR 115 yards (105 meters)
- ☐ Dk Purple (Color B) - 1 skein
  OR 30 yards (27.5 meters)

Crochet Hook

- ☐ Size G (4 mm)
  or size needed for gauge

Additional Supplies

- ☐ Yarn needle

GAUGE INFORMATION

In chart pattern,
16 sc and 18 rows = 4" (10 cm)

Gauge Swatch: 4" (10 cm) square

Ch 17.

Row 1: Sc in second ch from hook and in each ch across.

Rows 2-18: Ch 1, turn; sc in each sc across.

Finish off.

Note: Entire dishcloth is made with sc ***(see Basic Stitches, page 47)***.

DISHCLOTH

With Color A, ch 46.

Row 1 (Right side): Sc in second ch from hook and in each ch across: 45 sc.

Note: Loop a short piece of yarn around any stitch to mark Row 1 as **right** side.

Rows 2-6: Ch 1, turn; sc in each sc across.

To change colors, work sc **before** color change to the last step (2 loops on hook), yarn over with the new color and draw through both loops on hook ***(Fig. A)***, dropping the old color. Work over dropped color as you work the row ***(Fig. B)***.

Fig. A

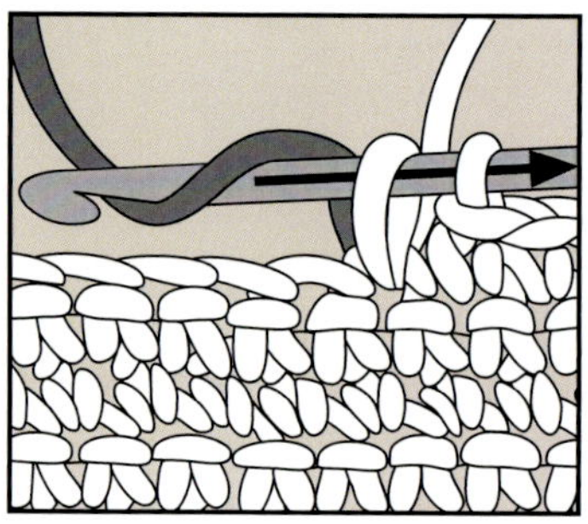

Fig. B

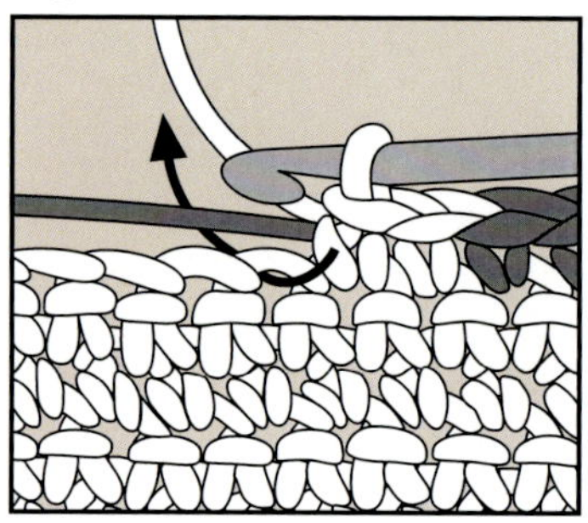

Row 7: Ch 1, turn; sc in first 14 sc changing to Color B in last sc, with Color B sc in next 3 sc changing to Color A in last sc, with Color A sc in next sc changing to Color B, with Color B sc in next 3 sc, with Color A sc in next 4 sc, with Color B sc in next 2 sc, with Color A sc in next 2 sc, with Color B sc in next sc, with Color A sc in last 15 sc.

Rows 8-45: Following Chart on page 16 for color changes, continue to work in sc; cut Color B after working Row 40; do **not** finish off.

Trim

Rnd 1: With Color A ch 1, do **not** turn; working in end of rows, skip first row, sc in next 43 rows, skip last row; working in free loops of beginning ch ***(Fig. 1, page 47)***, 3 sc in first ch, sc in next 43 chs, 3 sc in next ch; working in end of rows, skip first row, sc in next 43 rows, skip last row; 3 sc in first sc of Row 45, sc in next 43 sc, 3 sc in last sc; join with slip st to first sc, finish off: 184 sc.

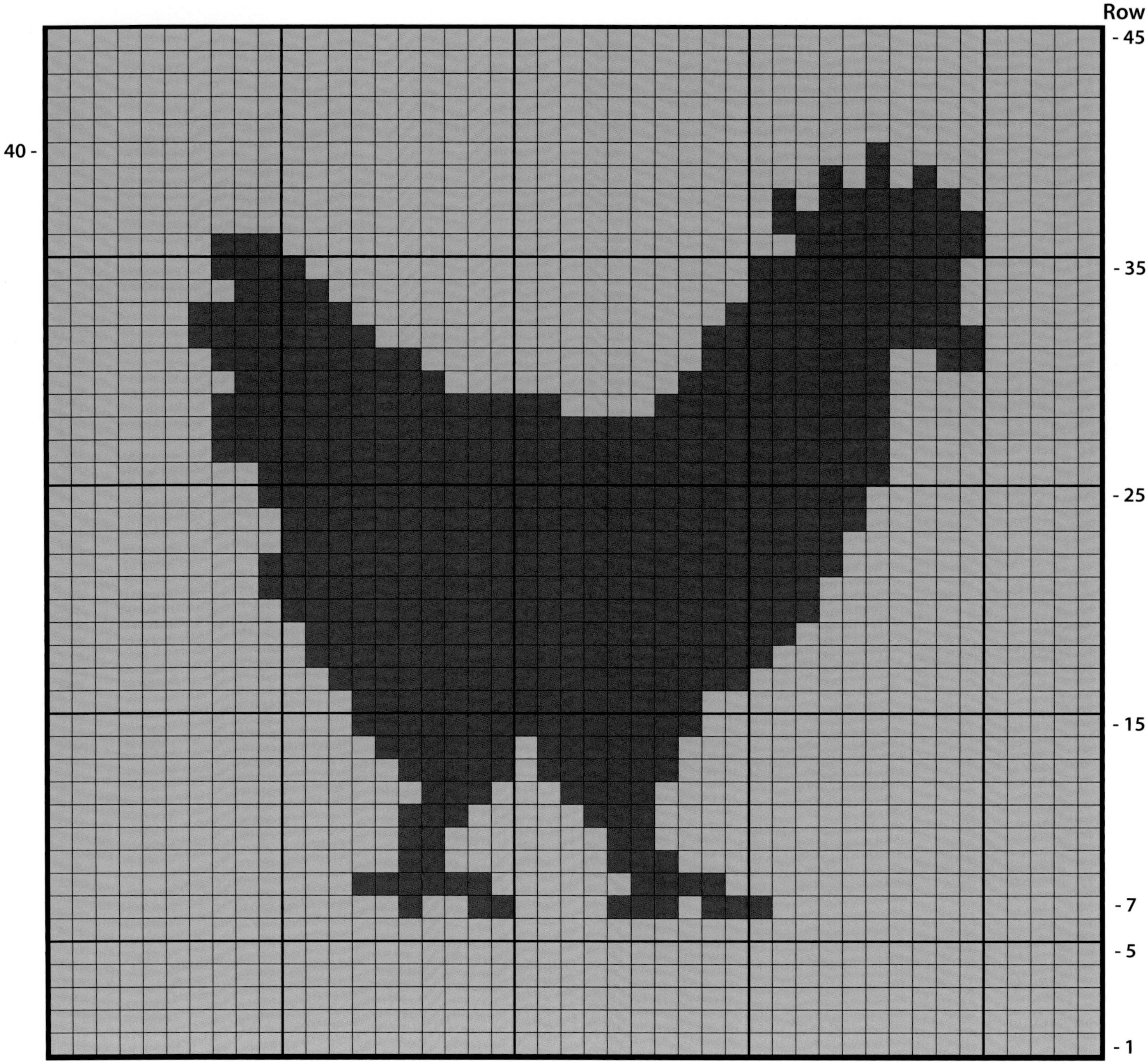

CHART

Work from **right** to **left** on right side rows; work from **left** to **right** on wrong side rows.

KEY

Color A

Color B

Cheesy Chicken

Recipe from Mary Maxwell

Prep Time: 15 minutes

Need a fast dinner...so you can crochet more? I've got you covered with this easy cheesy pasta!

Directions:

1. In a large pot, bring the broth to a gentle boil. Add butter to melt.
2. Add pasta, salt and pepper to broth, continue to boil until pasta is tender. Drain.
3. Add chicken, cream cheese, Veg-All and parsley to pasta and mix until melted.
4. Remove from heat; let stand 5-10 minutes.

Ingredients:

4 (14.5 ounce) cans chicken broth
2 tablespoon butter
1 (16 ounce) box pasta
Salt and pepper to taste
1 lb diced cooked chicken
1 (8 ounce) package cream cheese
1 (15 ounce) can Veg·All® or mixed vegetables
2 teaspoons chopped parsley

Makes about 6 servings

Flower

●●○○ EASY

Finished Size:
Approximately 10½" (26.5 cm) square

SHOPPING LIST

Yarn (Medium Weight) MEDIUM 4

[2.65 ounces, 131 yards (75 grams, 120 meters) per skein]:

- ☐ Cream (Color A) - 1 skein
  OR 110 yards (100.5 meters)
- ☐ Dk Pink (Color B) - 1 skein
  OR 35 yards (32 meters)
- ☐ Lime Green (Color C) - 1 skein
  OR 10 yards (9 meters)

Crochet Hook

- ☐ Size G (4 mm)
  or size needed for gauge

Additional Supplies

- ☐ Yarn needle

GAUGE INFORMATION

In chart pattern,
16 sc and 18 rows = 4" (10 cm)

Gauge Swatch: 4" (10 cm) square

Ch 17.

Row 1: Sc in second ch from hook and in each ch across.

Rows 2-18: Ch 1, turn; sc in each sc across.

Finish off.

Note: Entire dishcloth is made with sc ***(see Basic Stitches, page 47)***.

DISHCLOTH

With Color A, ch 46.

Row 1 (Right side): Sc in second ch from hook and in each ch across: 45 sc.

Note: Loop a short piece of yarn around any stitch to mark Row 1 as **right** side.

Rows 2-5: Ch 1, turn; sc in each sc across.

To change colors, work sc **before** color change to the last step (2 loops on hook), yarn over with the new color and draw through both loops on hook ***(Fig. A)***, dropping the old color. Work over dropped color as you work the row ***(Fig. B)***.

Fig. A

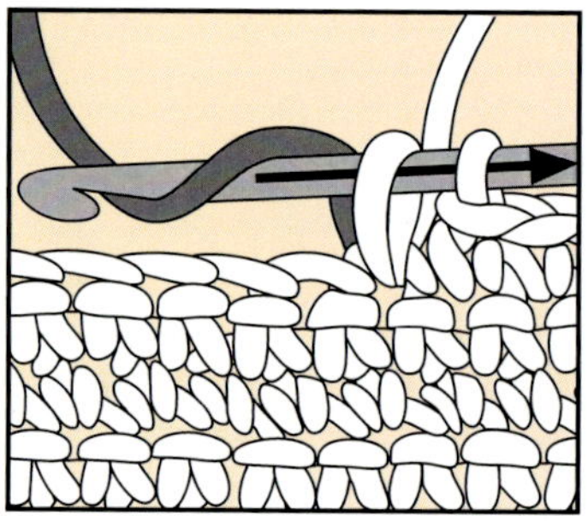

Fig. B

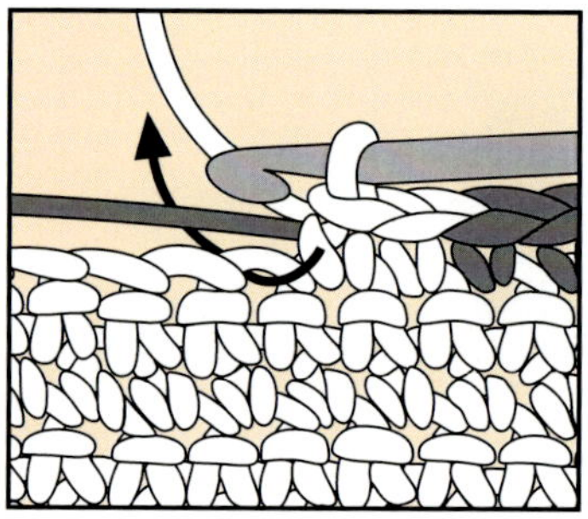

Row 6: Ch 1, turn; sc in first 6 sc changing to Color C in last sc, with Color C sc in next sc changing to Color A, with Color A sc in last 38 sc.

Rows 7-45: Following Chart on page 20 for color changes, continue to work in sc; cut Color B and Color C after working Row 38; do **not** finish off.

Trim

Rnd 1: With Color A ch 1, do **not** turn; working in end of rows, skip first row, sc in next 43 rows, skip last row; working in free loops of beginning ch ***(Fig. 1, page 47)***, 3 sc in first ch, sc in next 43 chs, 3 sc in next ch; working in end of rows, skip first row, sc in next 43 rows, skip last row; 3 sc in first sc of Row 45, sc in next 43 sc, 3 sc in last sc; join with slip st to first sc, finish off: 184 sc.

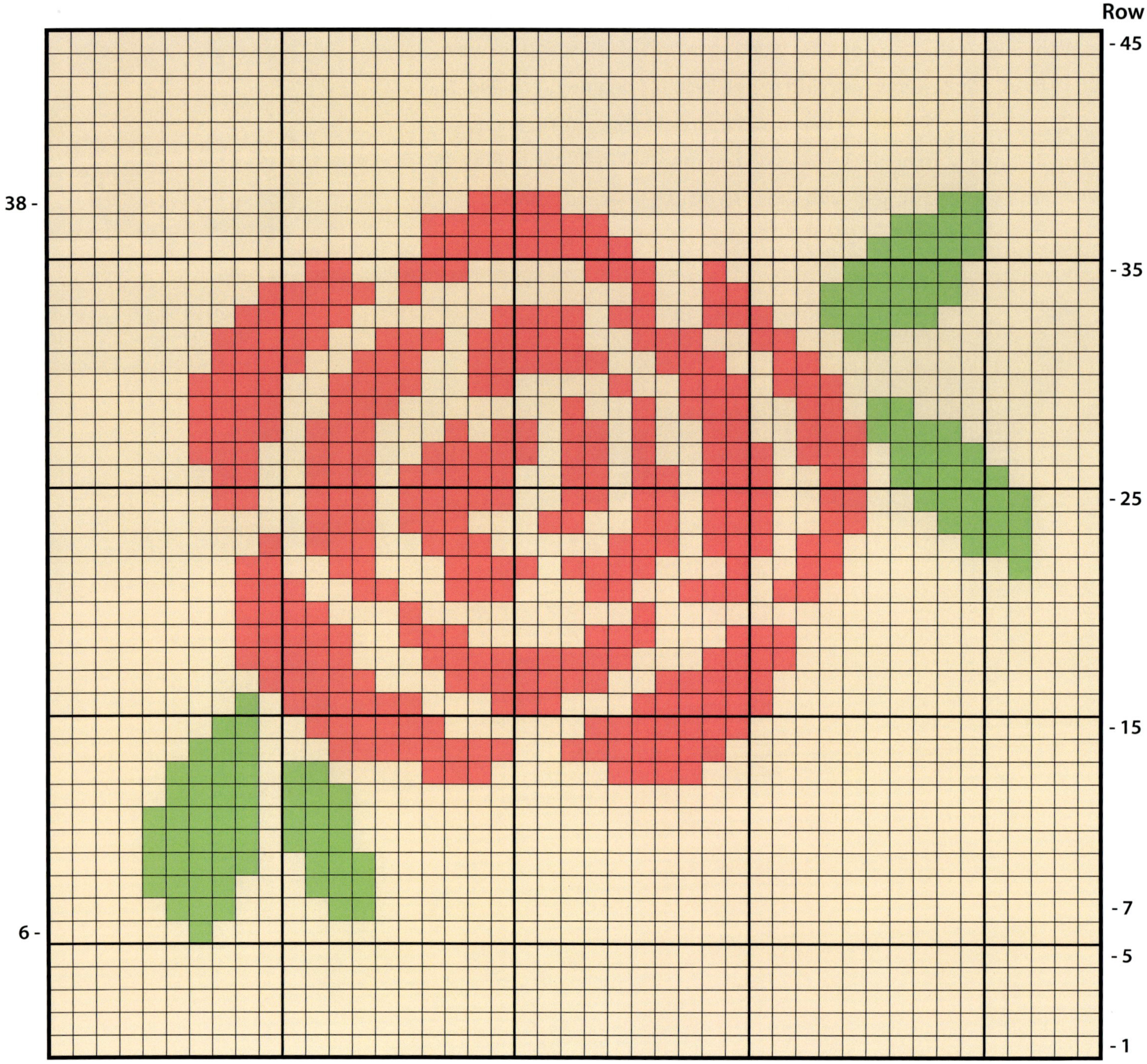

CHART

Work from **right** to **left** on right side rows; work from **left** to **right** on wrong side rows.

KEY

Color A

Color B

Color C

Squash & Zucchini Casserole

Recipe from Mary Maxwell

Prep Time: 15 minutes

This may be my favorite recipe in the entire book...just because I love zucchini! This goes perfectly with the flower dishcloth because the plant blooms with a flower before it creates the squash! Any excuse to use zucchini!

Directions:

1. Preheat the oven to 350° fahrenheit.
2. Spray a 8" x 11" baking pan with cooking spray.
3. Bring a large pot of generously salted water to a boil. Combine squash, zucchini and onion and boil until tender. Drain thoroughly.
4. Crush crackers.
4. Add milk, 1 cup crushed crackers and ¾ cup cheese to the mixture.
5. Transfer to the prepared baking pan.
6. Add crushed crackers to the top of the mixture. Sprinkle with remaining cheese.
7. Bake for 15 minutes, or until the cheese is melted.
8. Store leftovers in a covered container in the refrigerator for up to 3 days.

Ingredients:

- 2 cups sliced yellow squash
- 1 cup sliced zucchini
- ½ cup diced onion
- ½ cup milk
- 1 sleeve saltine crackers
- 1 cup shredded cheddar cheese

Makes about 6 servings

Lemon

EASY

Finished Size:

Approximately 10½" (26.5 cm) square

SHOPPING LIST

Yarn (Medium Weight) MEDIUM 4

[2.65 ounces, 131 yards (75 grams, 120 meters) per skein]:

- ☐ Pink (Color A) - 1 skein
  OR 100 yards (91.5 meters)
- ☐ Yellow (Color B) - 1 skein
  OR 35 yards (32 meters)
- ☐ White (Color C) - 1 skein
  OR 30 yards (27.5 meters)

Crochet Hook

- ☐ Size G (4 mm)
  or size needed for gauge

Additional Supplies

- ☐ Yarn needle

GAUGE INFORMATION

In chart pattern,
16 sc and 18 rows = 4" (10 cm)

Gauge Swatch: 4" (10 cm) square

Ch 17.

Row 1: Sc in second ch from hook and in each ch across.

Rows 2-18: Ch 1, turn; sc in each sc across.

Finish off.

Note: Entire dishcloth is made with sc ***(see Basic Stitches, page 47)***.

DISHCLOTH

With Color A, ch 46.

Row 1 (Right side): Sc in second ch from hook and in each ch across: 45 sc.

Note: Loop a short piece of yarn around any stitch to mark Row 1 as **right** side.

Rows 2-6: Ch 1, turn; sc in each sc across.

To change colors, work sc **before** color change to the last step (2 loops on hook), yarn over with the new color and draw through both loops on hook ***(Fig. A)***, dropping the old color. Work over dropped color as you work the row ***(Fig. B)***.

Fig. A

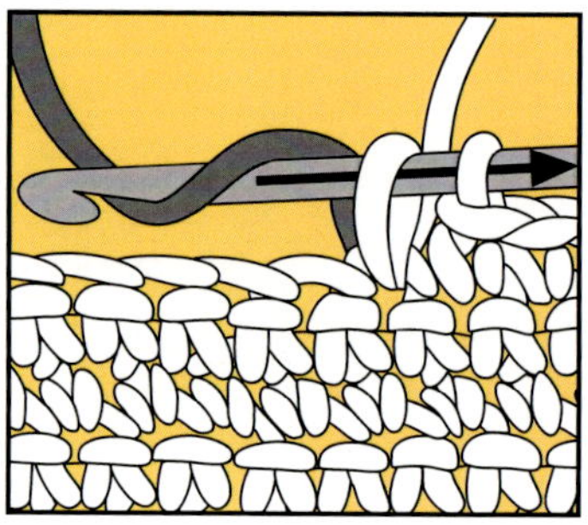

Fig. B

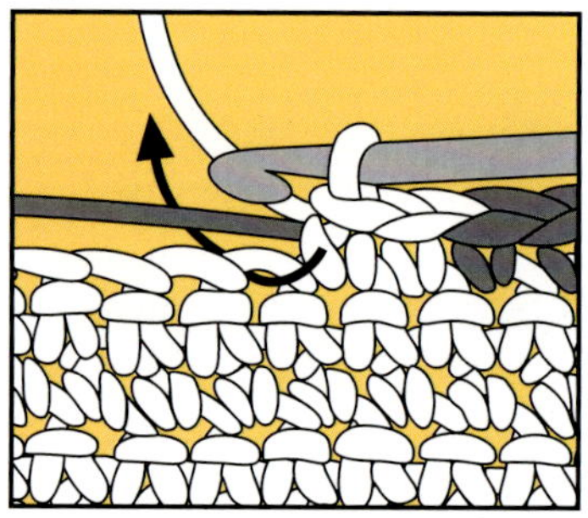

Row 7: Ch 1, turn; sc in first 17 sc changing to Color B in last sc, with Color B sc in next 10 sc changing to Color A in last sc, with Color A sc in last 18 sc.

Rows 8-45: Following Chart on page 24 for color changes, continue to work in sc; cut Color B after working Row 39; do **not** finish off.

Trim

Rnd 1: With Color A ch 1, do **not** turn; working in end of rows, skip first row, sc in next 43 rows, skip last row; working in free loops of beginning ch ***(Fig. 1, page 47)***, 3 sc in first ch, sc in next 43 chs, 3 sc in next ch; working in end of rows, skip first row, sc in next 43 rows, skip last row; 3 sc in first sc of Row 45, sc in next 43 sc, 3 sc in last sc; join with slip st to first sc, finish off: 184 sc.

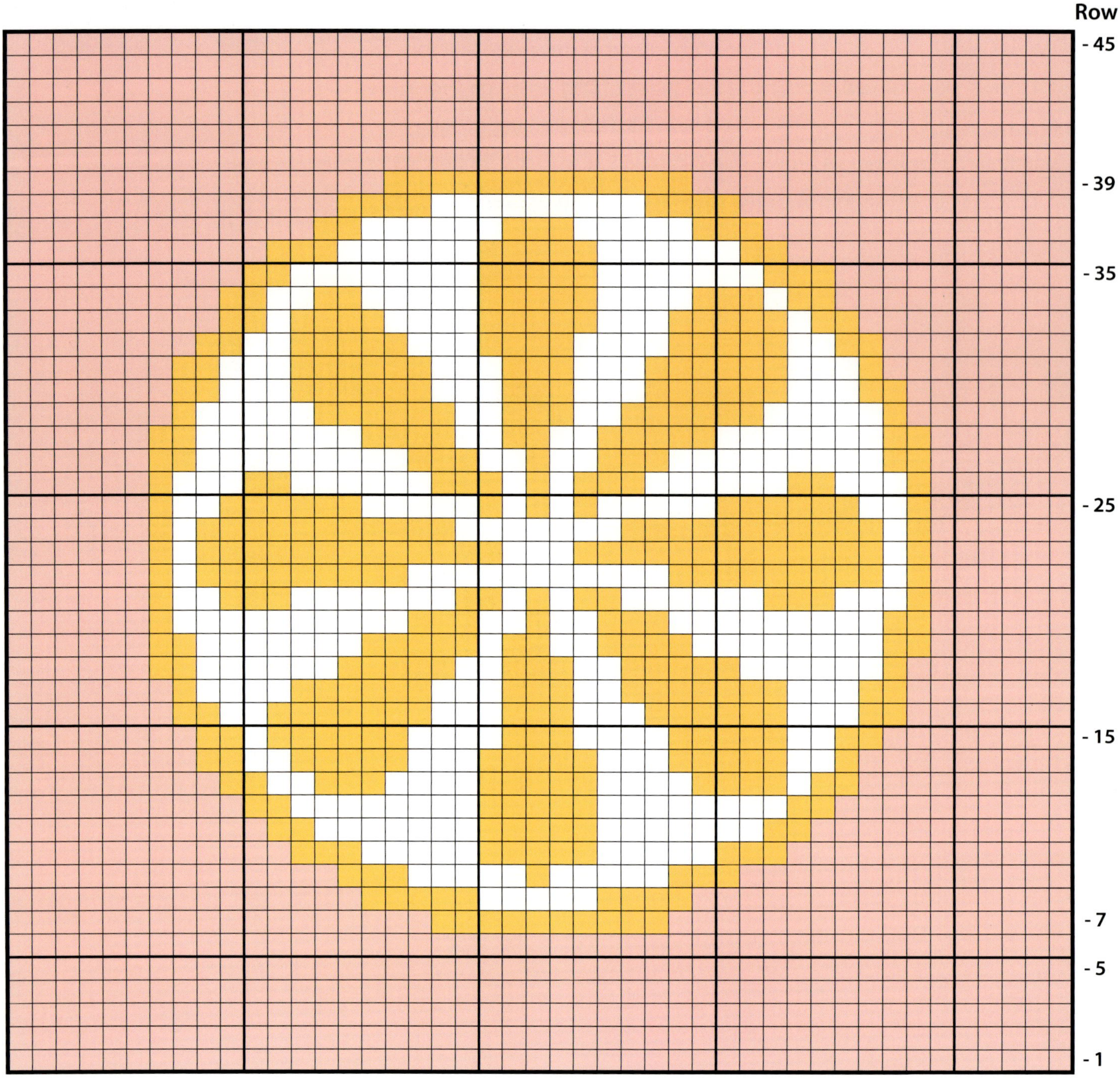

CHART

Work from **right** to **left** on right side rows; work from **left** to **right** on wrong side rows.

KEY

Color A

Color B

Color C

Sparkling Lemon-Lime Punch Lemonade

Recipe from Kristi Simpson

Prep Time: 5 minutes

As a child, one of our daughters made a fruity punch drink and was so proud. We would have to make it for all events! I love the idea of having kiddos help in the kitchen with easy recipes, so I took inspiration from her drink and brought you her fun punch! It's so simple...but it gives you that extra time to crochet.

Directions:

1. In a medium punch bowl, mix equal parts of lemon-lime drink and Fruit Punch.
2. Add sliced lemons, limes and strawberries for looks and taste.

Ingredients:

1 (2-liter) bottle Lemon-lime carbonated drink (I prefer Sprite®)

1 (59 ounce) carton of Minute Made® Fruit Punch

1 Lemon, sliced

1 Lime, sliced

½ pound (8 ounces) strawberries, sliced

Love

●●○○ EASY

Finished Size: Approximately 10½" (26.5 cm) square

SHOPPING LIST

Yarn (Medium Weight)

[2.65 ounces, 131 yards (75 grams, 120 meters) per skein]:

- ☐ Cream (Color A) - 1 skein **OR** 95 yards (87 meters)
- ☐ Red (Color B) - 1 skein **OR** 30 yards (27.5 meters)
- ☐ Lavender (Color C) - 1 skein **OR** 25 yards (23 meters)
- ☐ Green (Color D) - 1 skein **OR** 10 yards (9 meters)

Crochet Hook

- ☐ Size G (4 mm) **or** size needed for gauge

Additional Supplies

- ☐ Yarn needle

GAUGE INFORMATION

In chart pattern,
16 sc and 18 rows = 4" (10 cm)

Gauge Swatch: 4" (10 cm) square

Ch 17.

Row 1: Sc in second ch from hook and in each ch across.

Rows 2-18: Ch 1, turn; sc in each sc across.

Finish off.

Note: Entire dishcloth is made with sc *(see Basic Stitches, page 47)*.

DISHCLOTH

With Color A, ch 46.

Row 1 (Right side)**:** Sc in second ch from hook and in each ch across: 45 sc.

Note: Loop a short piece of yarn around any stitch to mark Row 1 as **right** side.

Rows 2 and 3: Ch 1, turn; sc in each sc across.

To change colors, work sc **before** color change to the last step (2 loops on hook), yarn over with the new color and draw through both loops on hook ***(Fig. A)***, dropping the old color. Work over dropped color as you work the row ***(Fig. B)***.

Fig. A

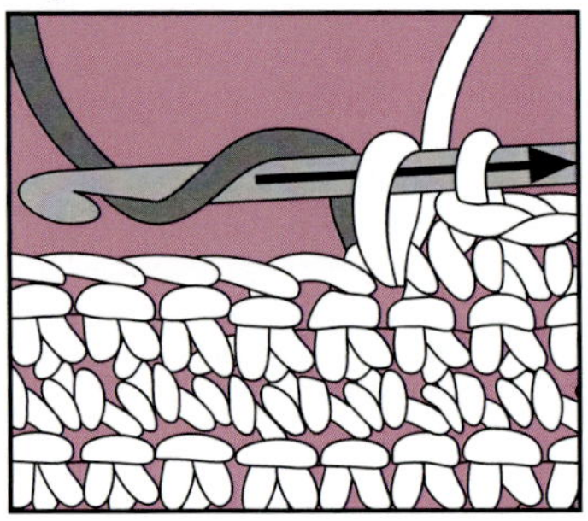

Fig. B

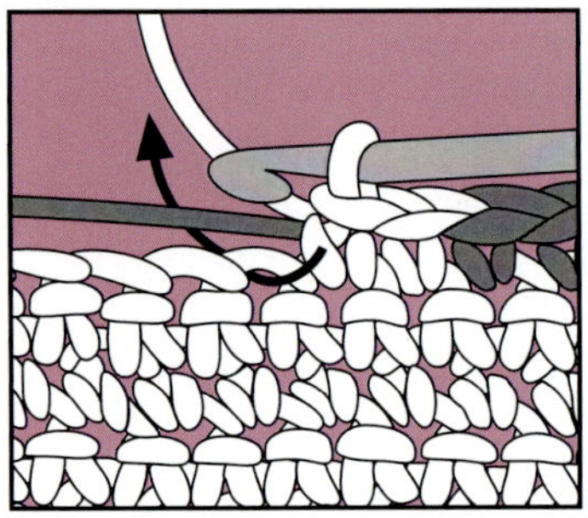

Row 4: Ch 1, turn; sc in first 11 sc changing to Color B in last sc, with Color B sc in next 6 sc changing to Color A in last sc, with Color A sc in next 8 sc, with Color C sc in next 12 sc, with Color A sc in last 8 sc.

Rows 5-45: Following Chart on page 28 for color changes, continue to work in sc; cut Color D after working Row 43; do **not** finish off.

Trim

Rnd 1: With Color A ch 1, do **not** turn; working in end of rows, skip first row, sc in next 43 rows, skip last row; working in free loops of beginning ch ***(Fig. 1, page 47)***, 3 sc in first ch, sc in next 43 chs, 3 sc in next ch; working in end of rows, skip first row, sc in next 43 rows, skip last row; 3 sc in first sc of Row 45, sc in next 43 sc, 3 sc in last sc; join with slip st to first sc, finish off: 184 sc.

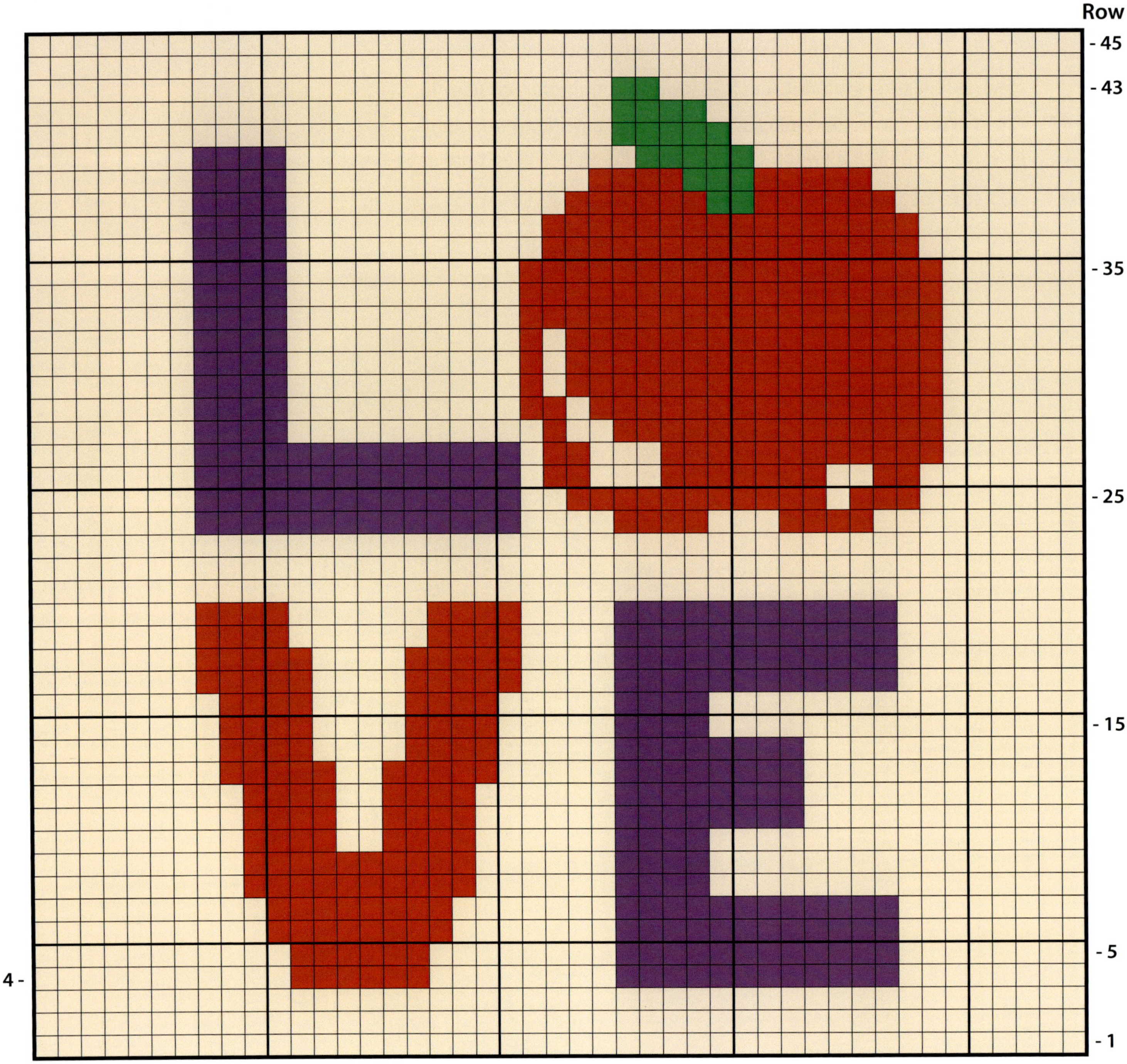

CHART

Work from **right** to **left** on right side rows; work from **left** to **right** on wrong side rows.

KEY

Color A

Color B

Color C

Color D

Mile High Apple Pie

Recipe from Kaye Goens

Prep Time: 15 minutes

Crochet and baking? Yes, please! This fun dishcloth paired with a yummy apple pie is perfect. How ever you eat your pie...with ice cream, whipped topping or straight from the fridge, this pie is sure to delight!

Directions:

1. Preheat the oven to 350° fahrenheit.
2. Toss sliced apples in lemon juice.
3. In a medium bowl, combine Splenda®, Splenda® brown sugar blend, cinnamon, salt and flour.
4. Toss apples in mixture to coat.
5. Roll out pie crust; place in a deep pie dish.
6. Pour apples in the center and dab butter on top of the apples.
7. Bring sides of pie crust up and over apples.
8. Whisk egg with 1 tablespoon of water for egg wash; brush crust with egg wash.
9. Sprinkle crust with cinnamon.
10. Bake for 1 hour.

Ingredients:

8 apples of your choice, peeled & sliced
2 tablespoons lemon juice
½ cup Splenda® granulated sugar substitute
⅓ cup Splenda® brown sugar blend
1½ teaspoon cinnamon
¼ teaspoon salt
¼ cup flour
1 package refrigerated pie crust
1 stick unsalted butter
1 large egg

Makes 6 to 8 servings

Mug

●●○○ EASY

finished Size:
Approximately 10½" (26.5 cm) square

SHOPPING LIST

Yarn (Medium Weight) MEDIUM 4

[2.65 ounces, 131 yards
(75 grams, 120 meters) per skein]:

- ☐ Black (Color A) - 1 skein
  OR 120 yards (110 meters)
- ☐ Cream (Color B) - 1 skein
  OR 30 yards (27.5 meters)

Crochet Hook

- ☐ Size G (4 mm)
  or size needed for gauge

Additional Supplies

- ☐ Yarn needle

GAUGE INFORMATION

In chart pattern,
16 sc and 18 rows = 4" (10 cm)

Gauge Swatch: 4" (10 cm) square

Ch 17.

Row 1: Sc in second ch from hook and in each ch across.

Rows 2-18: Ch 1, turn; sc in each sc across.

Finish off.

Note: Entire dishcloth is made with sc *(see Basic Stitches, page 47)*.

DISHCLOTH

With Color A, ch 46.

Row 1 (Right side): Sc in second ch from hook and in each ch across: 45 sc.

Note: Loop a short piece of yarn around any stitch to mark Row 1 as **right** side.

Rows 2-4: Ch 1, turn; sc in each sc across.

To change colors, work sc **before** color change to the last step (2 loops on hook), yarn over with the new color and draw through both loops on hook ***(Fig. A)***, dropping the old color. Work over dropped color as you work the row ***(Fig. B)***.

Fig. A

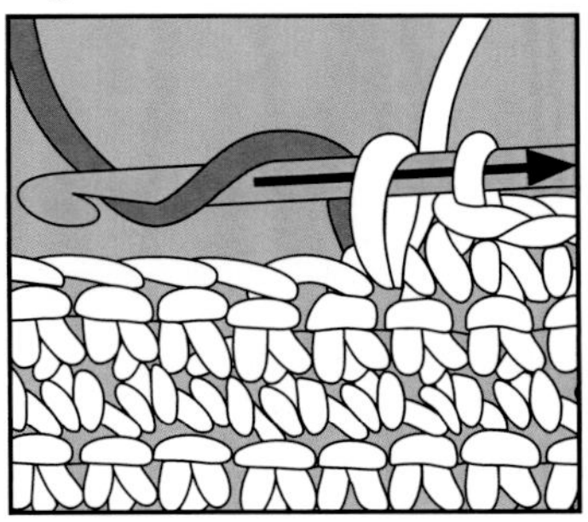

Fig. B

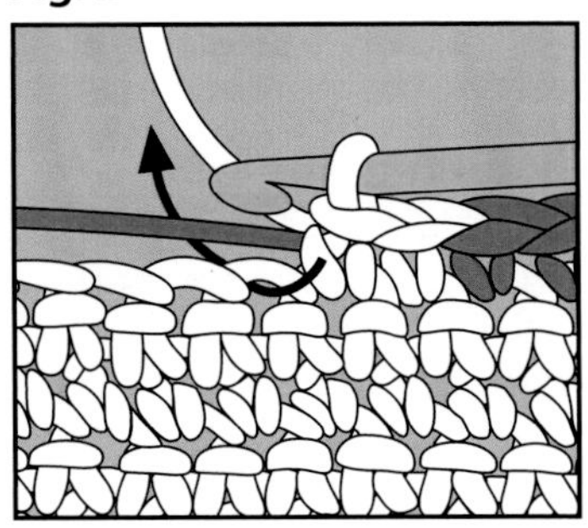

Row 5: Ch 1, turn; sc in first 15 sc changing to Color B in last sc, with Color B sc in next 18 sc changing to Color A in last sc, with Color A sc in last 12 sc.

Rows 6-45: Following Chart on page 32 for color changes, continue to work in sc; cut Color B after working Row 42; do **not** finish off.

Trim

Rnd 1: With Color A ch 1, do **not** turn; working in end of rows, skip first row, sc in next 43 rows, skip last row; working in free loops of beginning ch ***(Fig. 1, page 47)***, 3 sc in first ch, sc in next 43 chs, 3 sc in next ch; working in end of rows, skip first row, sc in next 43 rows, skip last row; 3 sc in first sc of Row 45, sc in next 43 sc, 3 sc in last sc; join with slip st to first sc, finish off: 184 sc.

Row

CHART

Work from **right** to **left** on right side rows; work from **left** to **right** on wrong side rows.

KEY

Color A

Color B

Hot Cocoa

Recipe from Kristi Simpson

Prep Time: 5 minutes

Are you a cocoa or coffee person? Maybe tea? Either route you choose, this mug cloth is for you! Now, I love a good cup of hot cocoa! Skip the packs and make your own with this yummy recipe….don't forget the peppermint!

Directions:

1. In a medium saucepan, warm milk to a simmer (do not boil).
2. Whisk cocoa powder and sugar into milk until dissolved.
3. Add chocolate chips to the mixture and melt.
4. Add vanilla extract.
5. Top with whipped cream and crushed peppermint.

Ingredients:

4 cups milk
¼ cup unsweetened cocoa powder
¼ cup granulated sugar
½ cup semi-sweet chocolate chips (if using regular chocolate chips, it will make cocoa sweeter!)
1/8 teaspoon vanilla extract
Whipped cream
Peppermint, crushed

Makes 4 servings

Pear & Cherry

●●○○ EASY

Finished Size: Approximately 10½" (26.5 cm) square

SHOPPING LIST

Yarn (Medium Weight) MEDIUM 4

[2.65 ounces, 131 yards (75 grams, 120 meters) per skein]:

- ☐ White (Color A) - 1 skein
  OR 110 yards (100.5 meters)
- ☐ Red (Color B) - 1 skein
  OR 15 yards (13.5 meters)
- ☐ Sage Green (Color C) - 1 skein
  OR 15 yards (13.5 meters)
- ☐ Lime Green (Color D) - 1 skein
  OR 35 yards (32 meters)

Crochet Hook

- ☐ Size G (4 mm)
  or size needed for gauge

Additional Supplies

- ☐ Yarn needle

GAUGE INFORMATION

In chart pattern,
16 sc and 18 rows = 4" (10 cm)

Gauge Swatch: 4" (10 cm) square
Ch 17.

Row 1: Sc in second ch from hook and in each ch across.

Rows 2-18: Ch 1, turn; sc in each sc across.

Finish off.

Note: Entire dishcloth is made with sc ***(see Basic Stitches, page 47)***.

DISHCLOTH

With Color A, ch 46.

Row 1 (Right side): Sc in second ch from hook and in each ch across: 45 sc.

Note: Loop a short piece of yarn around any stitch to mark Row 1 as **right** side.

Rows 2-4: Ch 1, turn; sc in each sc across.

To change colors, work sc **before** color change to the last step (2 loops on hook), yarn over with the new color and draw through both loops on hook ***(Fig. A)***, dropping the old color. Work over dropped color as you work the row ***(Fig. B)***.

Fig. A

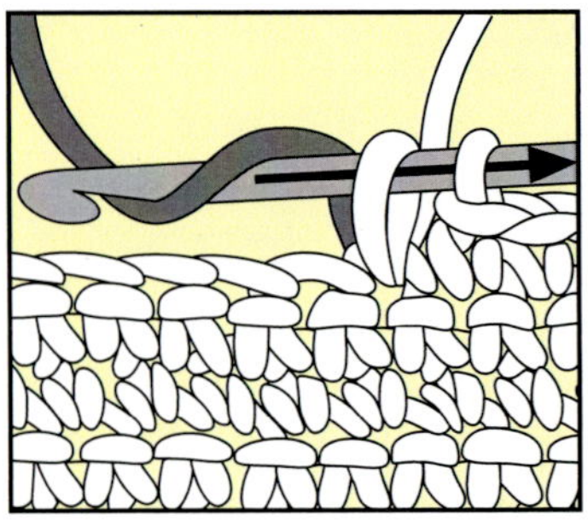

Fig. B

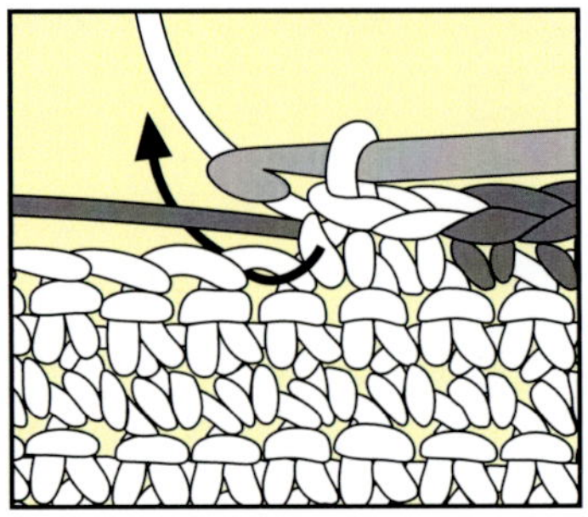

Row 5: Ch 1, turn; sc in first 22 sc changing to Color D in last sc, with Color D sc in next 10 sc changing to Color A in last sc, with Color A sc in last 13 sc.

Rows 6-45: Following Chart on page 36 for color changes, continue to work in sc; cut Color C after working Row 42; do **not** finish off.

Trim

Rnd 1: With Color A ch 1, do **not** turn; working in end of rows, skip first row, sc in next 43 rows, skip last row; working in free loops of beginning ch ***(Fig. 1, page 47)***, 3 sc in first ch, sc in next 43 chs, 3 sc in next ch; working in end of rows, skip first row, sc in next 43 rows, skip last row; 3 sc in first sc of Row 45, sc in next 43 sc, 3 sc in last sc; join with slip st to first sc, finish off: 184 sc.

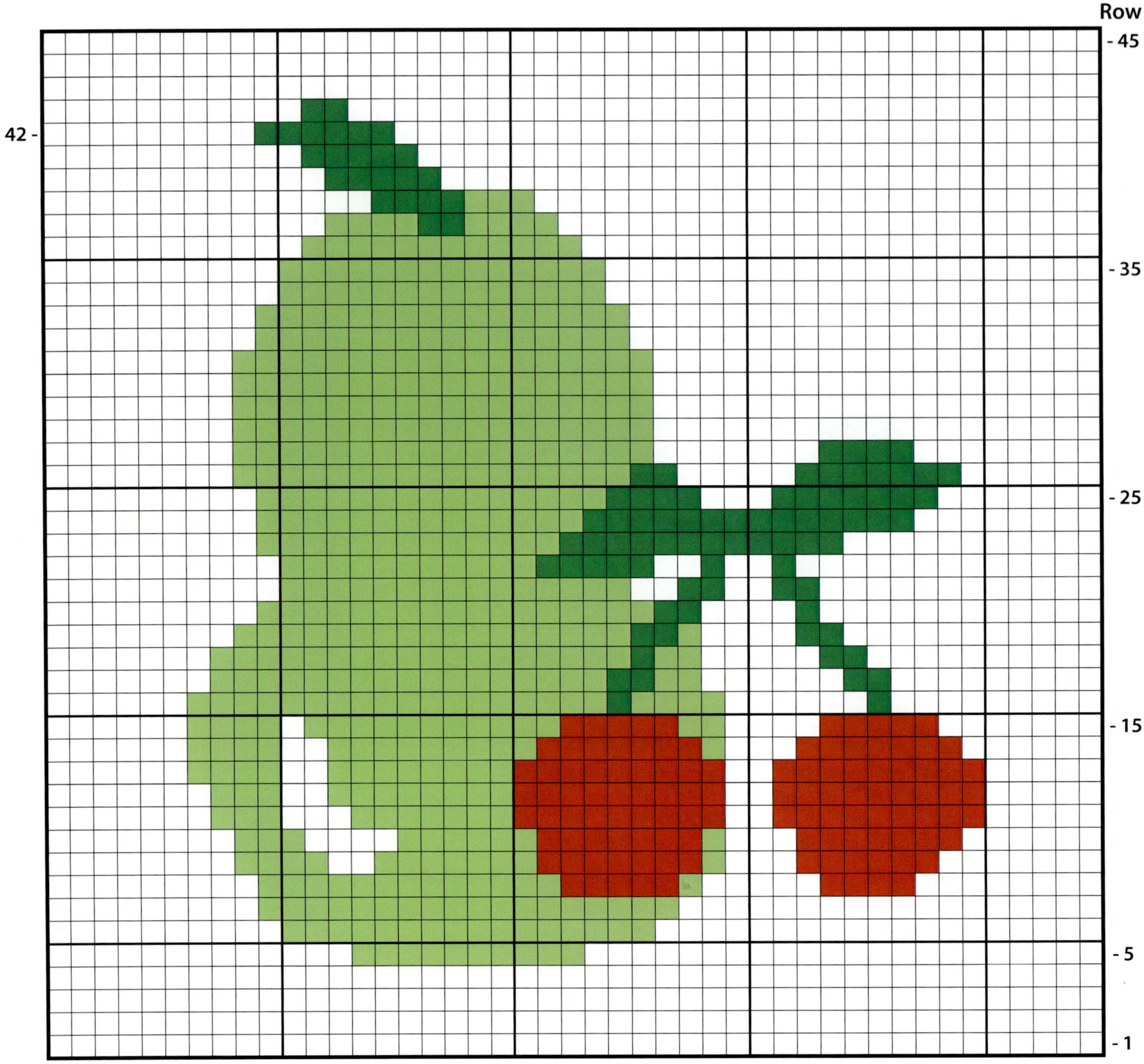

CHART

Work from **right** to **left** on right side rows; work from **left** to **right** on wrong side rows.

KEY

Color A

Color B

Color C

Color D

Pear Salad

Recipe from Kaye Goens

Prep Time: 10 minutes

This retro looking dish is beyond yummy. The dishcloth is so fun and 'cherry'...I mean cheery! Use this recipe as a side or a fun treat and keep 'em coming!

Directions:

1. Place lettuce leaves on serving plate.
2. Place pear halves on leaves.
3. Stir 2 teaspoons of shredded cheese into mayonnaise.
4. Place 1 teaspoon of this mix in center of each pear.
5. Sprinkle remaining cheddar cheese on top of mayonnaise.
6. Top with a cherry half if desired.

Ingredients:

- 1 (15 ounce) can pear halves (drained and chilled)
- 5 teaspoons mayonnaise (I prefer Hellmann's®)
- 7 teaspoons shredded cheddar cheese, divided
- 5-8 maraschino cherry halves (one for each pear), drained (optional)
- 2 or 3 curly lettuce leaves (optional for display)

Pork

●●○○ **EASY**

Finished Size: Approximately 10½" (26.5 cm) square

SHOPPING LIST

Yarn (Medium Weight)

[2.65 ounces, 131 yards
(75 grams, 120 meters) per skein]:

- ☐ Lt Blue (Color A) - 1 skein
  OR 120 yards (110 meters)
- ☐ Peach (Color B) - 1 skein
  OR 30 yards (27.5 meters)

Crochet Hook

- ☐ Size G (4 mm)
  or size needed for gauge

Additional Supplies

- ☐ Yarn needle

GAUGE INFORMATION

In chart pattern,
16 sc and 18 rows = 4" (10 cm)

Gauge Swatch: 4" (10 cm) square

Ch 17.

Row 1: Sc in second ch from hook and in each ch across.

Rows 2-18: Ch 1, turn; sc in each sc across.

Finish off.

Note: Entire dishcloth is made with sc ***(see Basic Stitches page 47)***.

DISHCLOTH

With Color A, ch 46.

Row 1 (Right side): Sc in second ch from hook and in each ch across: 45 sc.

Note: Loop a short piece of yarn around any stitch to mark Row 1 as **right** side.

Rows 2-13: Ch 1, turn; sc in each sc across.

To change colors, work sc **before** color change to the last step (2 loops on hook), yarn over with the new color and draw through both loops on hook ***(Fig. A)***, dropping the old color. Work over dropped color as you work the row ***(Fig. B)***.

Fig. A

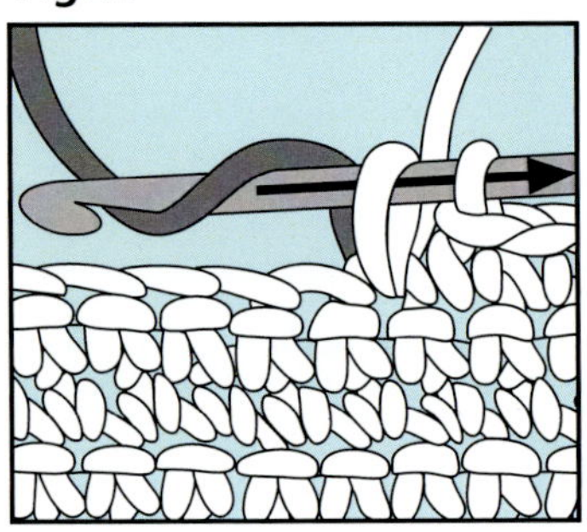

Fig. B

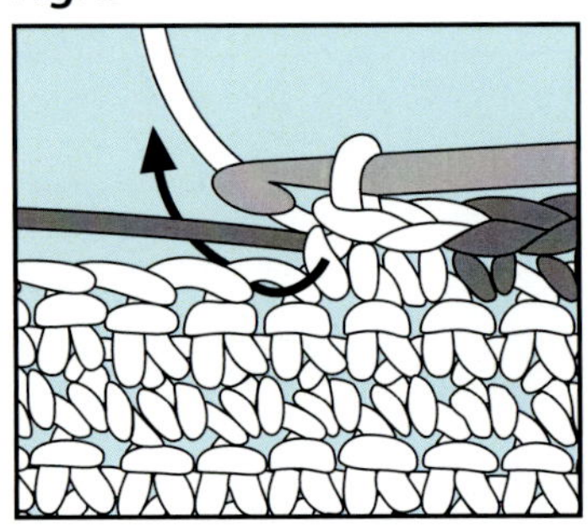

Row 14: Ch 1, turn; sc in first 8 sc changing to Color B in last sc, with Color B sc in next 3 sc changing to Color A in last sc, with Color A sc in next 2 sc, with Color B sc in next 2 sc, with Color A sc in next 10 sc, with Color B sc in next 2 sc, with Color A sc in next sc, with Color B sc in next 2 sc, with Color A sc in last 15 sc.

Rows 15-45: Following Chart on page 40 for color changes, continue to work in sc; cut Color B after working Row 33; do **not** finish off.

Trim

Rnd 1: With Color A ch 1, do **not** turn; working in end of rows, skip first row, sc in next 43 rows, skip last row; working in free loops of beginning ch ***(Fig. 1, page 47)***, 3 sc in first ch, sc in next 43 chs, 3 sc in next ch; working in end of rows, skip first row, sc in next 43 rows, skip last row; 3 sc in first sc of Row 45, sc in next 43 sc, 3 sc in last sc; join with slip st to first sc, finish off: 184 sc.

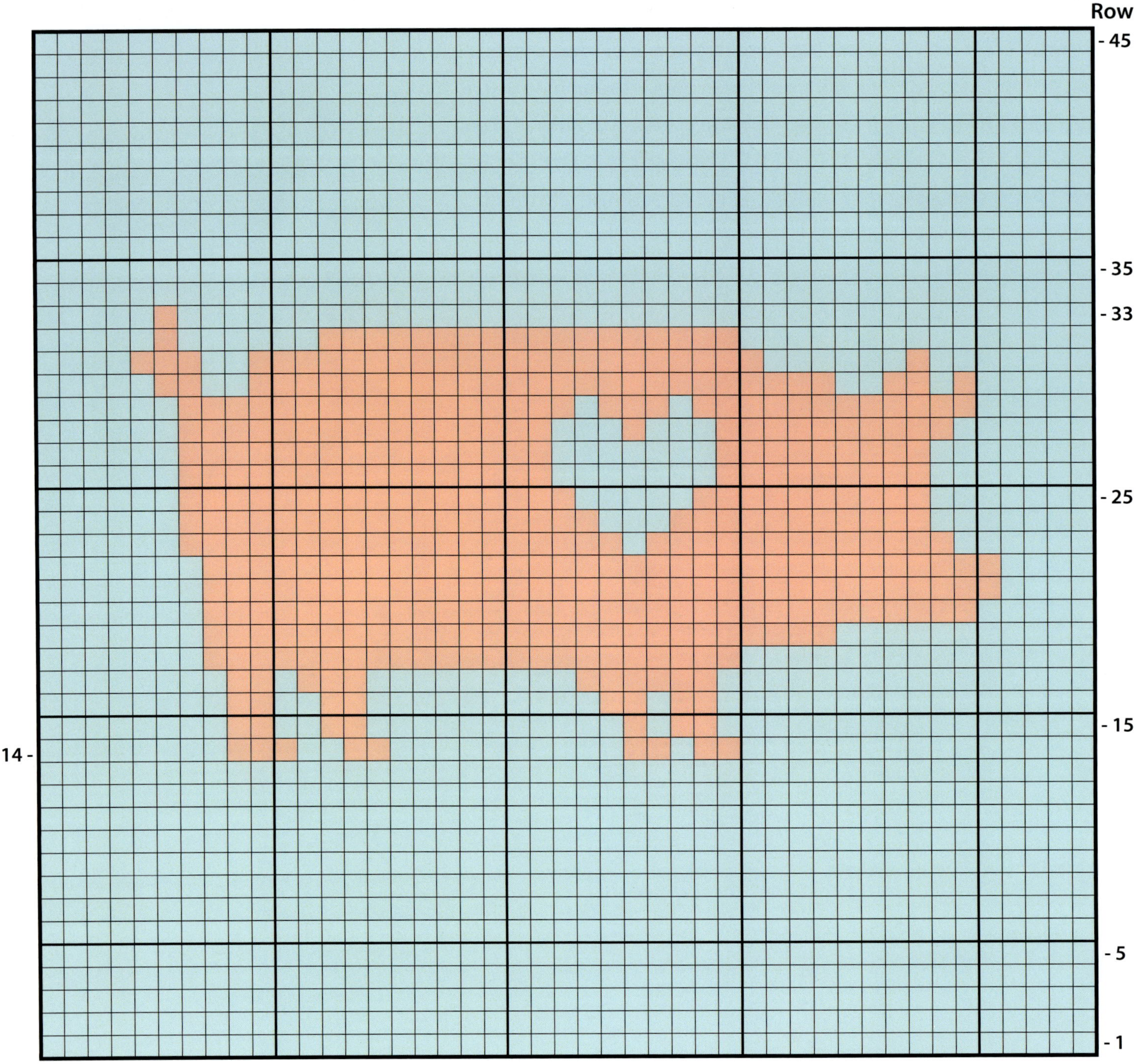

CHART

Work from **right** to **left** on right side rows; work from **left** to **right** on wrong side rows.

KEY

Color A

Color B

Sausage Balls

Recipe from Faye Forton

Prep Time: 10 minutes

If you're looking for a make-ahead breakfast or side dish, then you're going to love these simple sausage balls. They are sausage-y and cheesy and oh so Yummy! Pair them with the honey mustard dipping sauce (page 13) and it's the perfect late night snack….you're welcome!

Directions:

1. Preheat the oven to 400° fahrenheit.
2. Spray the baking sheet with cooking spray.
3. In a large bowl, mix all ingredients with hands until well combined.
4. Using 2 teaspoons, form a small ball and place on a baking pan.
5. Place the baking sheet in the oven uncovered and bake until light brown; about 20-25 minutes.

Ingredients:

- 1 pound sausage
- 1½ cups shredded cheddar cheese
- 1 drop of maple flavoring (optional)
- 2 large eggs
- 2½ cups self rising flour
- 2 tablespoons milk

Makes 30-35 sausage balls.

Yum

EASY

Finished Size:
Approximately 10½" (26.5 cm) square

SHOPPING LIST

Yarn (Medium Weight)

[2.65 ounces, 131 yards (75 grams, 120 meters) per skein]:

- ☐ Aqua (Color A) - 1 skein
  OR 100 yards (91 meters)
- ☐ White (Color B) - 1 skein
  OR 30 yards (27.5 meters)

Crochet Hook

- ☐ Size G (4 mm)
  or size needed for gauge

Additional Supplies

- ☐ Yarn needle

GAUGE INFORMATION

In chart pattern,
16 sc and 18 rows = 4" (10 cm)

Gauge Swatch: 4" (10 cm) square

Ch 17.

Row 1: Sc in second ch from hook and in each ch across.

Rows 2-18: Ch 1, turn; sc in each sc across.

Finish off.

Note: Entire dishcloth is made with sc ***(see Basic Stitches, page 47)***.

DISHCLOTH

With Color A, ch 46.

Row 1 (Right side)**:** Sc in second ch from hook and in each ch across: 45 sc.

Note: Loop a short piece of yarn around any stitch to mark Row 1 as **right** side.

Rows 2-9: Ch 1, turn; sc in each sc across.

To change colors, work sc **before** color change to the last step (2 loops on hook), yarn over with the new color and draw through both loops on hook ***(Fig. A)***, dropping the old color. Work over dropped color as you work the row ***(Fig. B)***.

Fig. A

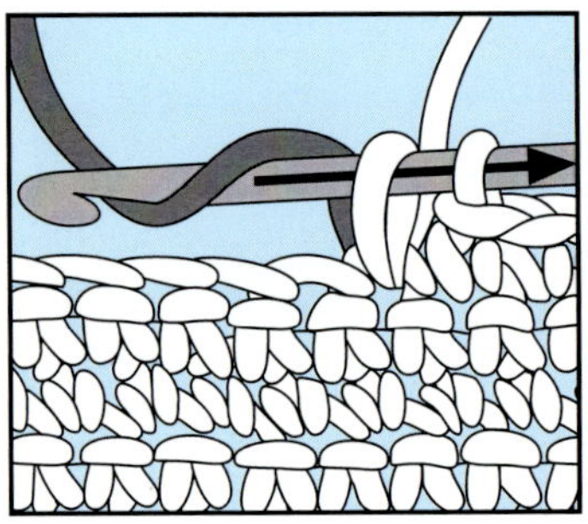

Fig. B

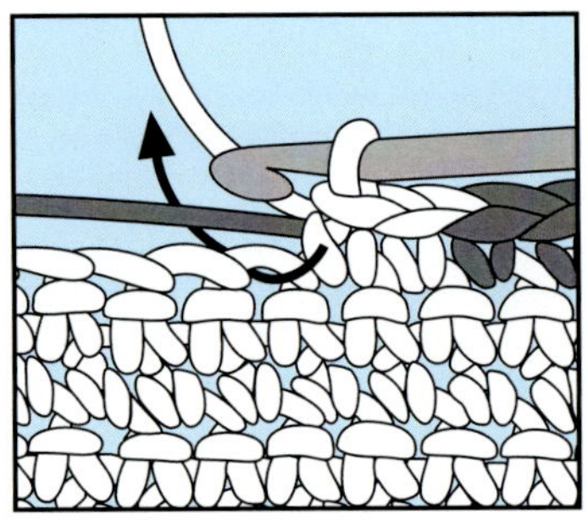

Row 10: Ch 1, turn; sc in first 10 sc changing to Color B in last sc, with Color B sc in next 4 sc changing to Color A in last sc, with Color A sc in last 31 sc.

Rows 11-45: Following Chart on page 44 for color changes, continue to work in sc; cut Color B after working Row 37; do **not** finish off.

Trim

Rnd 1: With Color A ch 1, do **not** turn; working in end of rows, skip first row, sc in next 43 rows, skip last row; working in free loops of beginning ch ***(Fig. 1, page 47)***, 3 sc in first ch, sc in next 43 chs, 3 sc in next ch; working in end of rows, skip first row, sc in next 43 rows, skip last row; 3 sc in first sc of Row 45, sc in next 43 sc, 3 sc in last sc; join with slip st to first sc, finish off: 184 sc.

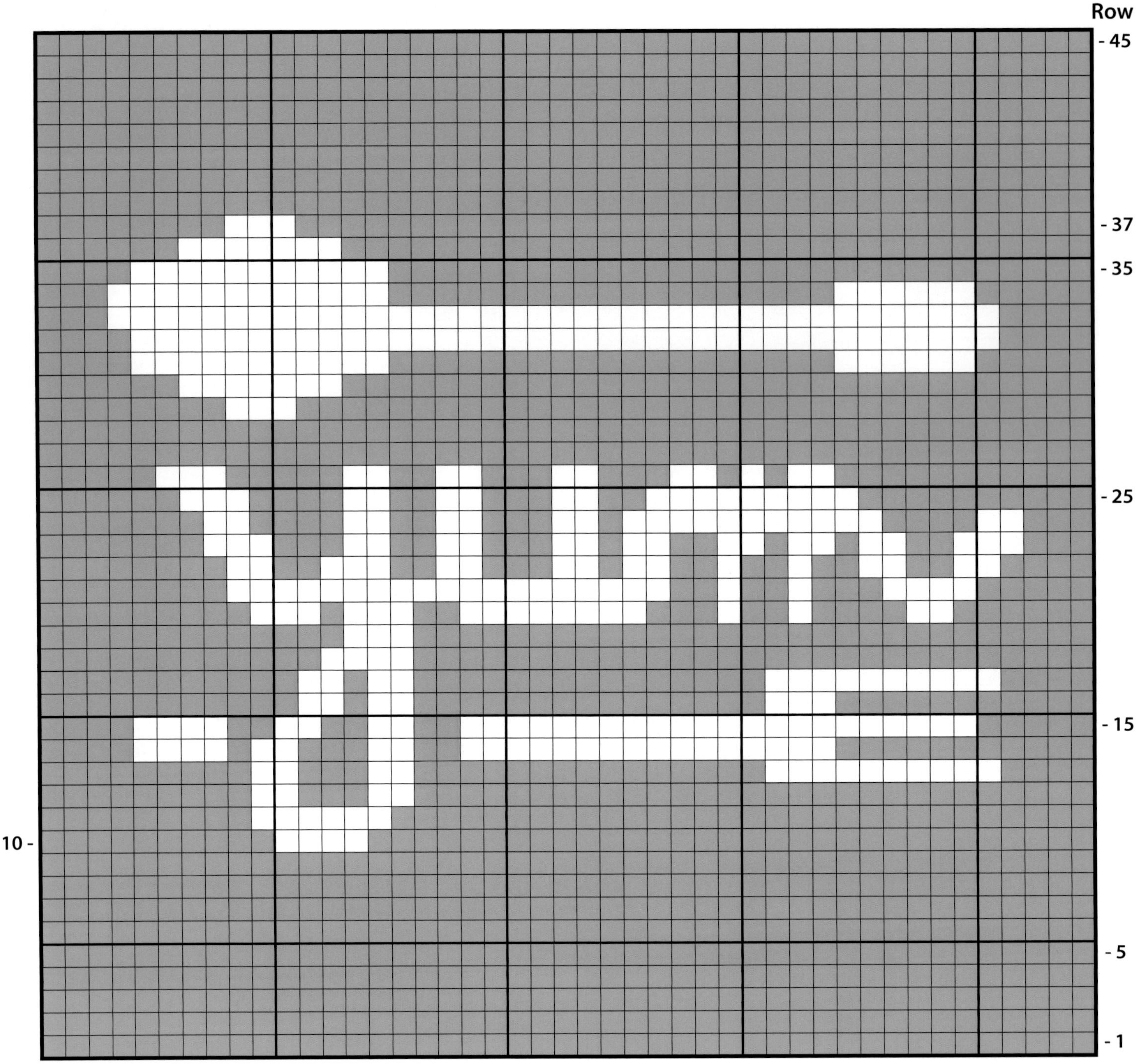

CHART

Work from **right** to **left** on right side rows; work from **left** to **right** on wrong side rows.

KEY

Color A (gray)

Color B (white)

Beef Stroganoff

Recipe from Kaye Goens

Prep Time: 15 minutes

Stick me with a fork. I'm done. And you will be too after this yummy dinner! This is a great beefy go-to and it's easier to make homemade than ever with this recipe. Match this fun YUM dishcloth with any décor and recipe and enjoy!

Directions:

1. Sprinkle salt and pepper on steak, then dust with flour.
2. In a medium skillet, add olive oil and butter. When hot, add steak to it. Brown steak on both sides. Remove steak from the skillet.
3. In the same skillet, add onion slices and sliced mushrooms and sauté until tender; about 1 to 2 minutes. Sprinkle onions and mushrooms with flour and place steak back in the pan.
4. Add cream of mushroom soup and beef broth to the skillet. Cook on low heat about 25 minutes, adjusting seasoning to taste.
5. Stir in sour cream and cook 5 minutes.
6. Add cooked noodles to the mixture and stir.

Ingredients:

1½ pounds thinly sliced steak
Salt and pepper to taste
¼ cup flour
2 tablespoons olive oil
2 tablespoons butter
1 medium onion, sliced
8 ounces fresh white mushrooms, sliced
1 (10.75 ounce) can cream of mushroom soup
1 (10.75 ounce) can beef broth
1 cup sour cream
1 package egg noodles, cooked

Makes about 6 servings.

General Instructions

ABBREVIATIONS

ch(s)	chain(s)
cm	centimeters
mm	millimeters
Rnd(s)	Round(s)
sc	single crochet(s)
st(s)	stitch(es)

SYMBOLS & TERMS

( ) or [ ] — contains explanatory remarks.

colon (:) — the number(s) given after a colon at the end of a row or round denote(s) the number of stitches you should have on that row or round.

CROCHET TERMINOLOGY		
UNITED STATES		INTERNATIONAL
slip stitch (slip st)	=	single crochet (sc)
single crochet (sc)	=	double crochet (dc)
half double crochet (hdc)	=	half treble crochet (htr)
double crochet (dc)	=	treble crochet (tr)
treble crochet (tr)	=	double treble crochet (dtr)
double treble crochet (dtr)	=	triple treble crochet (ttr)
triple treble crochet (tr tr)	=	quadruple treble crochet (qtr)
skip	=	miss

GAUGE

Exact gauge is **essential** for proper size. Before beginning your Dishcloth, make the sample swatch given in the individual instructions in the yarn and hook specified. After completing the swatch, measure it, counting your stitches and rows carefully. If your swatch is larger or smaller than specified, **make another, changing hook size to get the correct gauge.** Keep trying until you find the size hook that will give you the specified gauge.

●○○○ BASIC	Projects using basic stitches. May include basic increases and decreases.
●●○○ EASY	Projects may include simple stitch patterns, color work, and/or shaping.
●●●○ INTERMEDIATE	Projects may include involved stitch patterns, color work, and/or shaping.
●●●● COMPLEX	Projects may include complex stitch patterns, color work, and/or shaping using a variety of techniques and stitches simultaneously.

Yarn Weight Symbol & Names	LACE 0	SUPER FINE 1	FINE 2	LIGHT 3	MEDIUM 4	BULKY 5	SUPER BULKY 6	JUMBO 7
Type of Yarns in Category	Fingering, size 10 crochet thread	Sock, Fingering, Baby	Sport, Baby	DK, Light Worsted	Worsted, Afghan, Aran	Chunky, Craft, Rug	Super Bulky, Roving	Jumbo, Roving
Crochet Gauge* Ranges in Single Crochet to 4" (10 cm)	32-42 sts**	21-32 sts	16-20 sts	12-17 sts	11-14 sts	8-11 sts	6-9 sts	5 sts and fewer
Advised Hook Size Range	Steel*** 6 to 8, Regular hook B-1	B-1 to E-4	E-4 to 7	7 to I-9	I-9 to K-10½	K-10½ to M/N-13	M/N-13 to Q	Q and larger

*GUIDELINES ONLY: The chart above reflects the most commonly used gauges and hook sizes for specific yarn categories.

** Lace weight yarns are usually crocheted with larger hooks to create lacy openwork patterns. Accordingly, a gauge range is difficult to determine. Always follow the gauge stated in your pattern.

*** Steel crochet hooks are sized differently from regular hooks–the higher the number, the smaller the

CROCHET HOOKS																
U.S.	B-1	C-2	D-3	E-4	F-5	G-6	7	H-8	I-9	J-10	K-10½	L-11	M/N-13	N/P-15	P/Q	Q	S
Metric - mm	2.25	2.75	3.25	3.5	3.75	4	4.5	5	5.5	6	6.5	8	9	10	15	16	19

BASIC STITCHES

FREE LOOPS OF A CHAIN

When instructed to work in free loops of a chain, work in the loop indicated by arrow *(Fig. 1)*.

Fig. 1

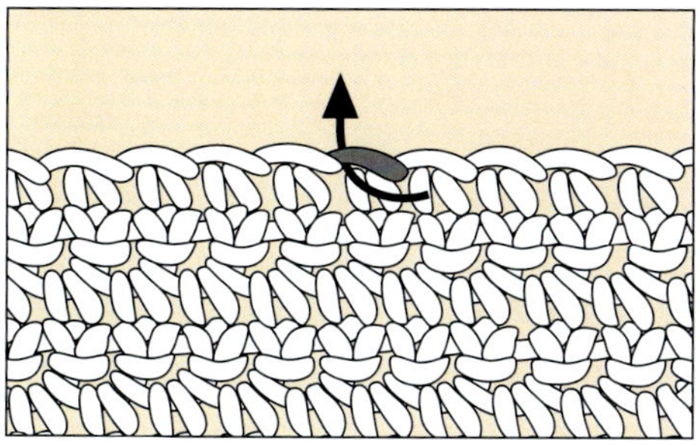

CHAIN

To work a chain stitch, begin with a slip knot on the hook. Bring the yarn over the hook from **back** to **front**, catching the yarn with the hook and turning the hook slightly toward you to keep the yarn from slipping off. Draw the yarn through the slip knot *(Fig. 2)* **(first chain stitch made, *abbreviated ch*)**.

Fig. 2

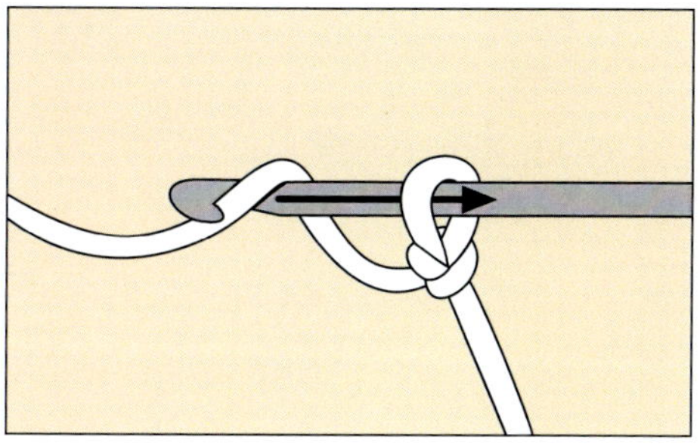

SLIP STITCH

To work a slip stitch, insert the hook in the stitch indicated, yarn over and draw through the stitch **and** through the loop on the hook *(Fig. 3)* **(slip stitch made, *abbreviated slip st*)**.

Fig. 3

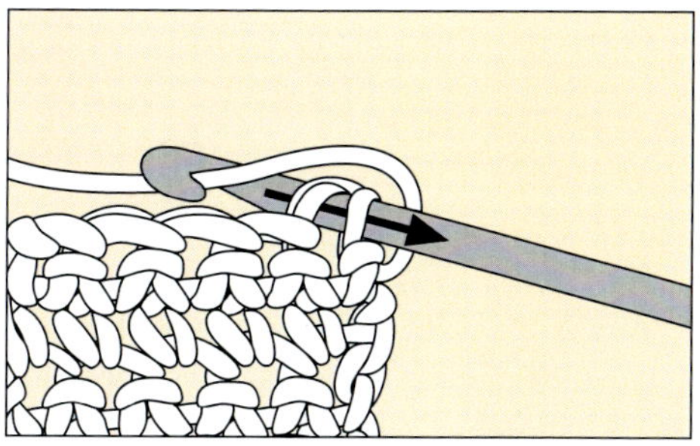

SINGLE CROCHET

Insert the hook in the stitch indicated, yarn over and pull up a loop, yarn over and draw through both loops on the hook *(Fig. 4)* **(single crochet made, *abbreviated sc*)**.

Fig. 4

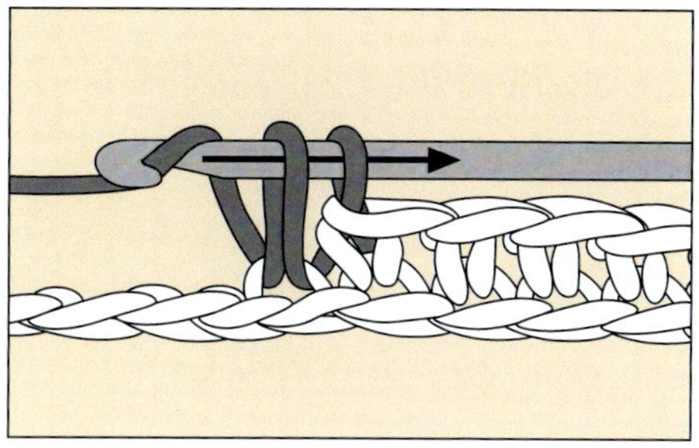

FINISH OFF

To finish off, cut the yarn leaving a 6" (15 cm) length. Bring the cut end of the yarn through the last loop *(Fig. 5)* and pull to tighten the stitch.

Fig. 5

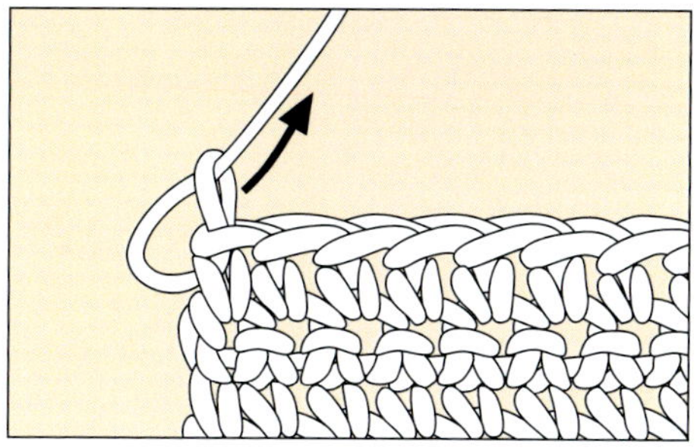

YARN INFORMATION

Each Dishcloth in this book was made using ***Premier Home***® cotton yarn. Any brand of Medium Weight yarn may be used. It is best to refer to the yardage/meters when determining how many balls or skeins to purchase. Remember, to arrive at the finished size, it is the GAUGE/TENSION that is important, not the brand of yarn.

For your convenience, listed below are the specific colors used to create our photography model. Because yarn manufacturers make frequent changes in their product lines, you may sometimes find it necessary to use a substitute yarn or to search for the discontinued product at alternate suppliers (locally or online).

BARN
- Color A: #38-02 Cream
- Color B: #38-23 Burgundy

BEE KIND
- Color A: #38-04 Yellow
- Color B: #38-16 Black

CHICKEN
- Color A: #38-26 Pewter
- Color B: #38-29 Eggplant

FLOWER
- Color A: #38-02 Cream
- Color B: #38-09 Fuchsia
- Color C: #38-21 Lime Green

LEMON
- Color A: #38-08 Pastel Pink
- Color B: #38-04 Yellow
- Color C: #38-01 White

LOVE
- Color A: #38-02 Cream
- Color B: #38-07 Cranberry
- Color C: #38-17 Passionfruit
- Color D: #38-14 Christmas Green

MUG
- Color A: #38-16 Black
- Color B: #38-02 Cream

PEAR & CHERRY
- Color A: #38-01 White
- Color B: #38-07 Cranberry
- Color C: #38-15 Sage (stems/leaf)
- Color D: #38-21 Lime Green (Pear)

PORK
- Color A: #38-13 Pastel Blue
- Color B: #38-05 Peach

YUM
- Color A: #38-12 Turquoise
- Color B: #38-01 White

Production Team: Publishing Manager - Megan Copeland; Project Manager/Technical Editor - Linda A. Daley; Graphic Artist - Michael Puckett; and Photographer - Rob Karman.

Made in U.S.A.